D1607161

Rita Santos

CHADWICK BOSEMAN

SUPERSTAR OF *BLACK PANTHER*

Enslow Publishing
101 W. 23rd Street
Suite 240
New York, NY 10011
USA

enslow.com

audition A tryout for a role.

biographical Having to do with the story of a person's life.

colonization Settling and taking control of a nation from its native people.

competition A contest for something.

dedicated Working hard at a task.

director The person in charge of actors and other people working on a movie.

playwright Someone who write plays.

recruit To actively encourage someone to join a group.

talent A natural skill or ability.

CONTENTS

Chadwick Boseman

As a little boy, Chadwick Boseman liked to read. He especially liked reading comic books. One of his favorite superheroes was Black Panther. Chadwick also liked to try new things. He found that he was good at many of the things he tried. He was a good student. He was a good artist. He was good at sports.

EARLY DAYS

Chadwick was born on November 29, 1977, in Anderson, South Carolina. His mother was a nurse. His father worked in a factory that made fabrics. He also ran a small business. Chadwick was close to both his parents.

Chadwick attended T. L. Hanna High School. Many people there noticed his many talents. They wondered

Chadwick Says:

"You practice to play in the big leagues."

As a young boy, Chadwick enjoyed reading about superheroes in comic books, especially *Black Panther*.

which one he would choose to pursue. Chadwick was recruited to play college basketball. He also loved to draw and wanted to become an architect. But everything changed when one of his teammates was killed in a random act of violence.

DISCOVERING THEATER

Chadwick had a difficult time when his teammate was killed. To deal with his feelings, he wrote a play. He got some friends together to perform it. He did act in the

Chadwick was on his town's 16-and-under AAU basketball team.

Chadwick graduated from Howard University in 2000. Eighteen years later, he went back to receive an honorary degree.

show, but he felt more like a **director** than an actor. In theater, directors have a very important role. They help actors understand the best ways to perform their roles. It was a powerful experience for Chadwick. He saw the impact writing and performing had on himself and his friends. "Suddenly, playing basketball wasn't as important," he said.

Chadwick decided to go to Howard University in Washington, DC. He wanted to study directing. Chadwick thought he'd finally chosen the path his life would follow. But life had more surprises in store for him.

CHAPTER 2
STUDYING TO BE A STAR

At Howard University, Chadwick was dedicated to his studies. He wanted to be the best writer and director he could be. He knew that to be a good director he would need to understand how his actors did their job. So he

decided to take an acting class. His teacher was actress Phylicia Rashad, best known for her role as Clair Huxtable on *The Cosby Show.* With her guidance, Chadwick realized he loved acting!

Phylicia Rashad was one of Chadwick's first drama teachers. She helped him figure out that he wanted to be an actor.

BECOMING AN ACTOR

Chadwick still wanted to write and direct. But he also knew he wanted to be onstage. He brought the same dedication to his acting that he brought to everything else. Chadwick's hard work paid off. He and some classmates were accepted into Oxford Summer Program of the British American Drama Academy in London. Unfortunately, the cost of the program and travelling overseas was too great for the students. They weren't sure they'd be able to go. Then Oscar-winning actor Denzel Washington stepped in. He was

Denzel Washington provided Chadwick and his classmates with the opportunity to study drama in London.

a friend of Phylicia Rashad. Denzel offered to pay for the students' admission to Oxford.

LEARNING HIS CRAFT

In London, Chadwick studied mainly white playwrights like William Shakespeare and Samuel Beckett. He wondered why black playwrights like August Wilson and Lorraine Hansberry weren't taught more often. He knew how important stories could be. He wondered why more weren't told about people that looked like him.

Chadwick Says:

"I always felt like black writers were just as classical."

Chadwick worked as a drama instructor for the New York Public Library.

After graduating from Howard, Chadwick moved to Brooklyn, New York. While living in New York, he attended New York City's Digital Film Academy. He continued to write and direct plays while going on auditions.

Acting is a very challenging career. But Chadwick felt very lucky to have the support of so many people. He was determined to make them proud.

Chapter 3
Making It in New York

When he was starting out, Chadwick had lots of luck landing small roles on television. He appeared on shows like *Third Watch*, *ER*, *Lincoln Heights*, and *Fringe*. But even though he was very talented, he had trouble finding larger roles. Chadwick was still determined to succeed. When he wasn't appearing on TV shows he continued writing plays with his friends.

Breakthrough

Chadwick's hard work finally paid off in 2012. He was cast as baseball legend Jackie Robinson in the movie *42*. The

Chadwick Says:
"I did whatever I could to stay in the groove of being an artist"

As a young actor, Chadwick knew he had to work hard to achieve success. His career began with several minor roles on television programs.

movie was about Robinson's life. He was the first African American to play in Major League Baseball. Chadwick took the role very seriously. It was a chance to tell an important story that was rarely heard.

Many people loved Chadwick's performance. Often, actors find it hard to play roles based on real people. But Chadwick enjoyed the challenge. Soon he was cast in

Chadwick performs as baseball great Jackie Robinson in the film *42*.

another biographical movie. He starred as soul singer James Brown in the film *Get on Up*. Brown was famous for his energetic dancing. Chadwick trained with a dance teacher for eight hours a day to get ready for the role. Once again his hard work paid off and audiences were pleased.

A DREAM ROLE

While Chadwick enjoyed the challenges of playing real people, there was one role he wanted most of all. Marvel

Chadwick once wrote a play that included a rapping Greek chorus.

After *42* was released, Chadwick and his costar Harrison Ford were invited to speak at the White House. Here, they listen to First Lady Michelle Obama speak. Also attending was Jackie Robinson's widow, Rachel.

Studios was looking for someone to be Black Panther. He longed to play the superhero he'd read about in comics as a child. The hero would have a small role in the movie *Captain America: Civil War*. He knew the competition for the role would be tough. He hoped he'd be allowed to audition for the role.

CHAPTER 4
BLACK PANTHER

One night while promoting a movie in Europe, Chadwick got a phone call. Marvel didn't want him to audition for the role of Black Panther. They had already chosen him for the role! Chadwick was so excited he wanted to share the news with his parents. But Marvel asked him to keep the news secret for a little while. It was a hard secret to keep!

CENTER STAGE

Captain America: Civil War came out in 2016. It was a big success. Even though Chadwick's role was small, audiences

Chadwick attends an event with his *Black Panther* costars, left to right: Danai Gurira, Lupita Nyong'o, and Michael B. Jordan.

wanted more. Marvel announced Black Panther would have his own movie in 2018. It would be the first movie to star a black superhero. Chadwick knew he had a big opportunity to tell another important story.

Black Panther is set in the fictional African nation of Wakanda. It was a country that had never been taken over by any other nation, which is known as colonization. Chadwick thought this was very important to the story. He says that colonization "doesn't just enslave the African…it enslaves everybody."

Chadwick Says:

"There's a lot of opportunity for magic to happen."

Chadwick's family can be traced back to Sierra Leone as well as the Yoruba people of Nigeria.

RUNAWAY HIT

Black Panther became one of the most watched movies of 2018. Audiences all over the world loved the movie. The film was culturally important because it was the first superhero movie to star an African American. It proved that a movie about African Americans could become popular with people of all backgrounds. Chadwick's dream had come true. Through his hard work and studies he was able to help tell a story that changed the world.

Chadwick walks the red carpet at the Academy Awards in 2018.

TIMELINE

1977 Chadwick is born on November 29 in Anderson, South Carolina.

1995 Graduates from T. L. Hanna High School.

2000 Earns a bachelor of arts in directing from Howard University.

2003 Lands first TV role on *Third Watch*.

2013 Stars in the movie *42*.

2014 Stars in the movie *Get on Up*.

2016 Is chosen to play King T'challa/Black Panther in *Captain America: Civil War*.

2018 Stars as King T'challa in the blockbuster film *Black Panther*.

LEARN MORE

BOOKS

Culver, Dennis. *Marvel's Black Panther: The Illustrated History of a King: The Complete Comics Chronology.* New York, NY: Insight Comics, 2018.

DiPrimio, Pete. *Chadwick Boseman.* Kennett Square, PA: Purple Toad, 2018

McCann, Jim. *MARVEL's Black Panther: The Junior Novel.* New York, NY: Little, Brown Books for Young Readers, 2018.

WEBSITES

Black Panther Official Movie Site

marvel.com/movies/black-panther

Read more about the character Black Panther's role in comic books and movies.

Chadwick Boseman

chadwick-boseman.com

Get the latest news, photos, and videos of Chadwick Boseman.

INDEX

Published in 2020 by Enslow Publishing, LLC.
101 W. 23rd Street, Suite 240, New York, NY 10011

Library of Congress Cataloging-in-Publication Data
Names: Santos, Rita, author.
Title: Chadwick Boseman : superstar of Black panther / Rita Santos.
Description: New York : Enslow Publishing, 2020. | Series: Junior biographies| Includes bibliographical references and index. | Audience: Grades 3-5.
Identifiers: LCCN 2018045963| ISBN 9781978507500 (library bound) | ISBN 9781978508774 (pbk.) | ISBN 9781978508781 (6 pack)
Subjects: LCSH: Boseman, Chadwick—Juvenile literature. | Actors—United States—Biography—Juvenile literature.
Classification: LCC PN2287.B645 S26 2018 | DDC 791.4302/8092 [B] —dc23
LC record available at https://lccn.loc.gov/2018045963

Printed in the United States of America

Photos Credits: Cover, p. 1 Alberto E. Rodriguez/Getty Images; p. 4 Albert L. Ortega/Getty Images; p. 6 Creative Stock/Alamy Stock Photo; p. 8 NurPhoto/Getty Images; p. 10 Paul Hawthorne/Getty Images; p. 11 Scott Gries/Getty Images; p. 15 Ray Mickshaw/WireImage/Getty Images; p. 16 Album/Alamy Stock Photo; p. 18 Alex Wong/Getty Images; p. 19 Han Myung-Gu/Getty Images; p. 20 Cindy Ord/Getty Images; p. 21 Frazer Harrison/Getty Images; interior page bottoms (film reels) thenatchdl/Shutterstock.com